CW00644052

First published in Edinburgh, Scotland
by Hide Press, 2022.

A CIP catalogue record for this book
is available from the British Library.

ISBN 978-1-3999-1812-1

the little book of

GINGERS

Kieran Dodds

Introduction

Despite appearances, this book is not really about hair, nor even a colour, for that matter. Over the last decade, I've been charting the travels of a rare – and incredibly photogenic – genetic trait visible in less than one per cent of the world's population.

The odds are far higher in Scotland, where one in eight people has red hair, although it's not really red, of course – not like blood or fire engines are. Instead, it spans a range of hues from deep peaty brown to coppery orange and bright shimmering gold. Recent findings suggest that this spectrum may be determined by variants on eight genes, including MC1R, the so-called 'ginger gene'. Forty per cent of the residents in Edinburgh are fortunate enough to be carriers of these MC1R variants, making the Scottish capital the world's brightest ginger hotspot.

Alexander Soued
Scotland
Age 6

The Little Book of Gingers extends far beyond the
Celtic fringe, though, transecting eleven time zones,
from the Americas, through Europe, and on to the
Middle East and Asia. In these portraits, you'll find,
among others, a Scottish boy with an Eastern European
mother and a Middle Eastern father (right), another
with an Indian great-grandfather (page 25) and
the famed 'Red People' of Treasure Beach, Jamaica
(pages 19, 39 and 49), where surnames reveal
not only Scottish heritage but also English, French
and Asian ancestry.

These people all have unique histories and live in
very different places. But they are united by a golden –
well, coppery, or rusty, as the Russians would say –
thread: the flow of DNA across cultures and generations.
The portraits are a reminder that humans are a wandering
species, that we are all made of the same substance,
and sometimes it shows.

Gilad Belkin
Israel
Age 27

Nixie Connelly
Scotland
Age 3

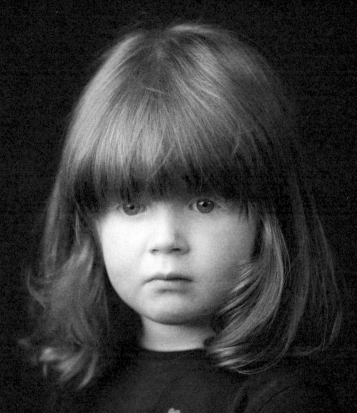

The Mackay family
Scotland

Steven
Age 36

Esther
Age 2

Rebecca
Age 33

Chloe
Age 8

Lois
Age 6

Abigail
Age 4

Jack McNaughton
Scotland
Age 10

Tatiana & Valeria Korotaeva
Russia
Ages 17 & 19

Thomasso Milazzo
Scotland
Age 2

Jordan DeLeon
Jamaica
Age 3

Ceara McVey
Scotland
Age 15

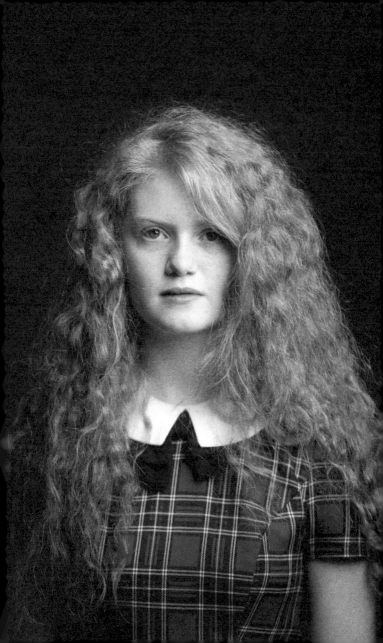

James Buswell
England
Age 27

Josh Hallam
Scotland
Age 11

Gwen Zipp
United States of America
Age 13

Dez Johnston
Scotland
Age 31

Margarita Bezukladnikova
Russia
Age 4

Rianne Wouda
Netherlands
Age 24

Nikolaj Loufbye
Denmark
Age 22

Sveta Ni
Russia
Age 21

Leon Swaby
Jamaica
Age 14

Dasha Shipitcina
Russia
Age 23

Pacey Young
Scotland
Age 15

John Ross
Scotland
Age 67

Lucy Fleming
Scotland
Age 12

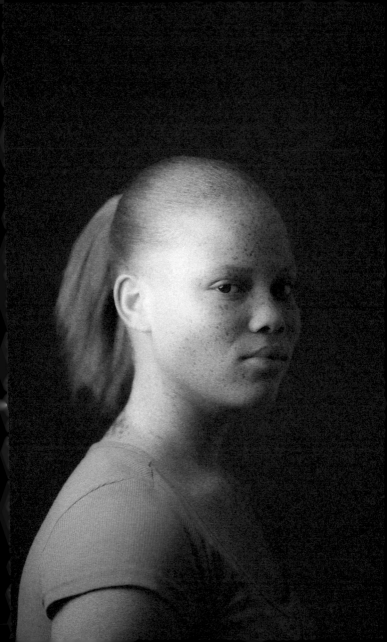

Isobel & Ada Dodds
Scotland
Age 2

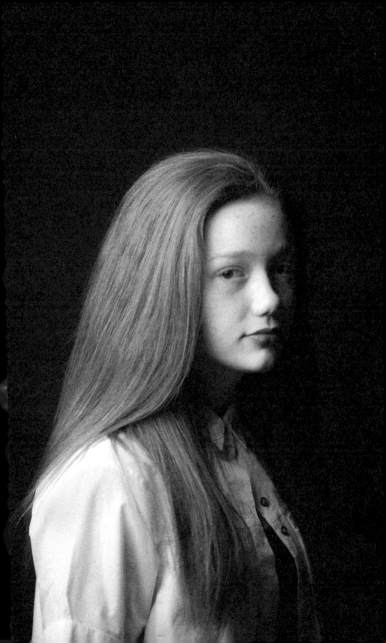

Marteka Nembhard
Jamaica
Age 14